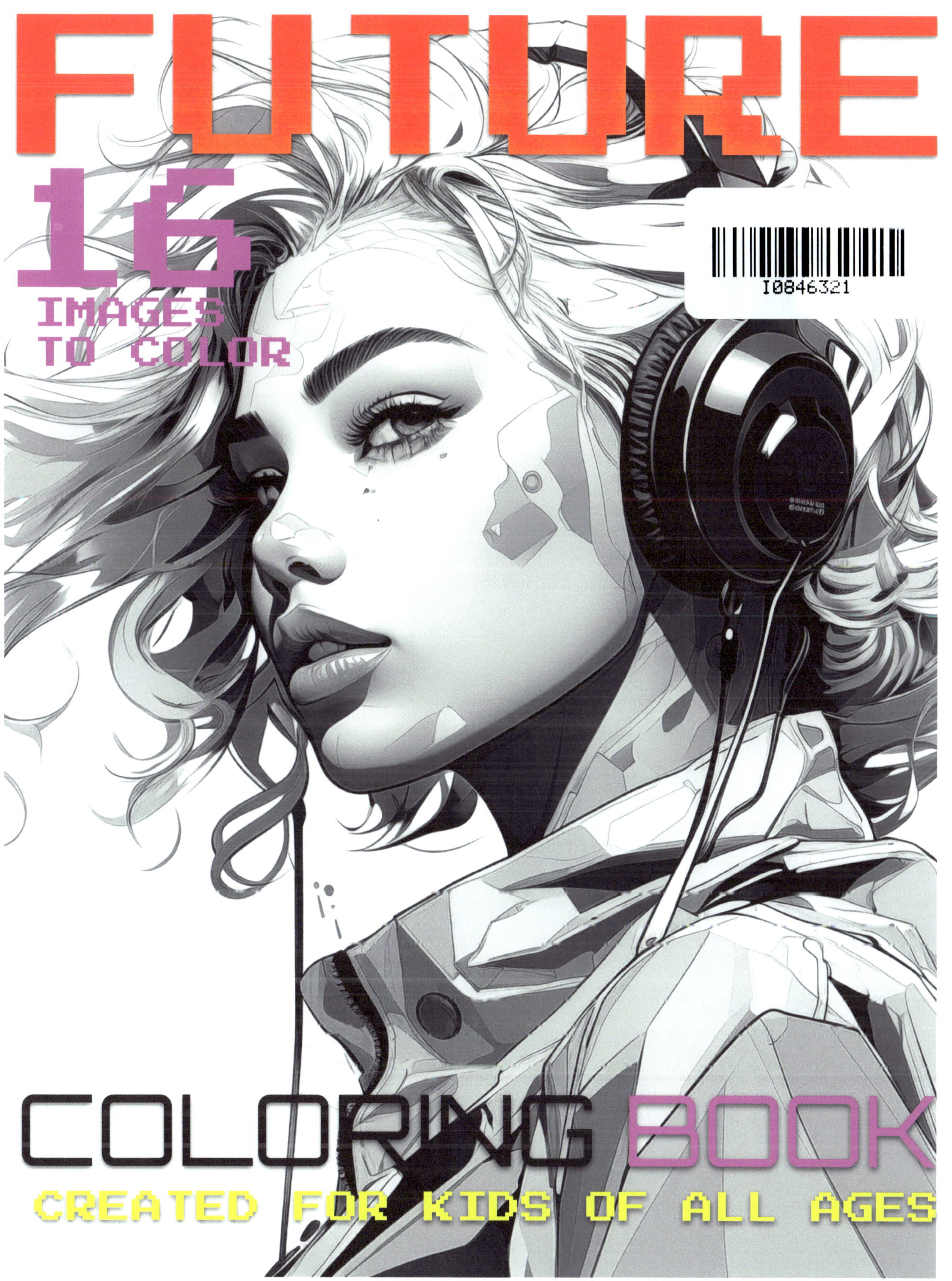
FUTURE
16
IMAGES
TO COLOR
I0846321
COLORING BOOK
CREATED FOR KIDS OF ALL AGES

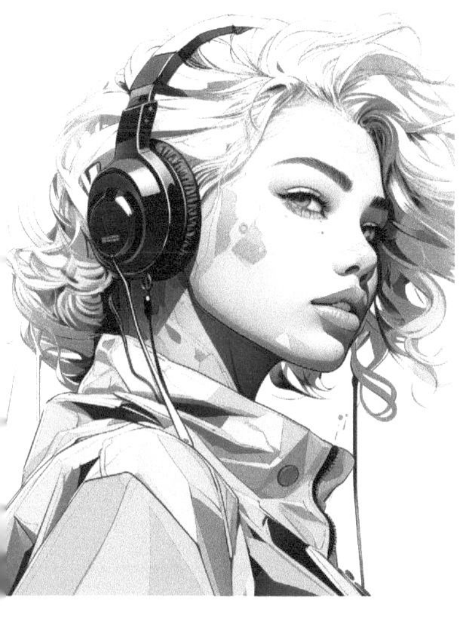
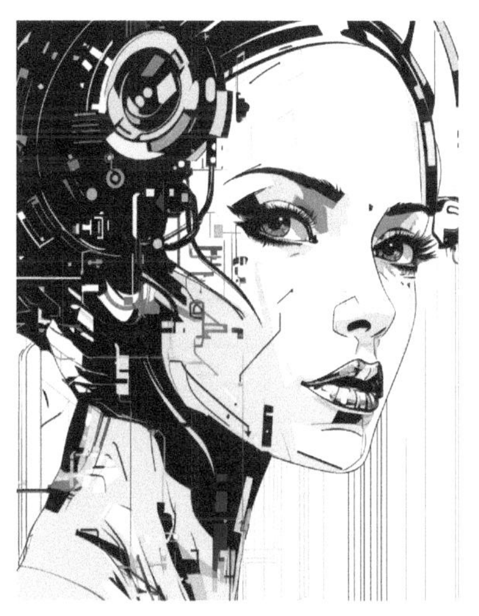
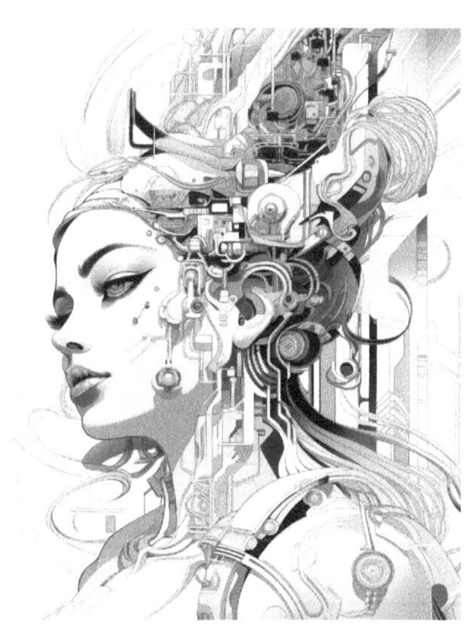
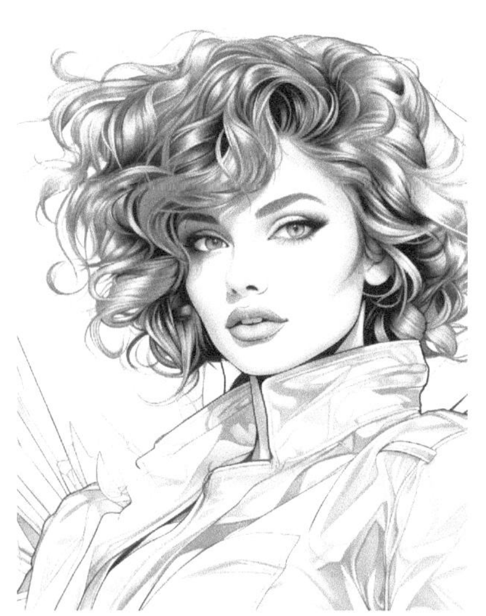
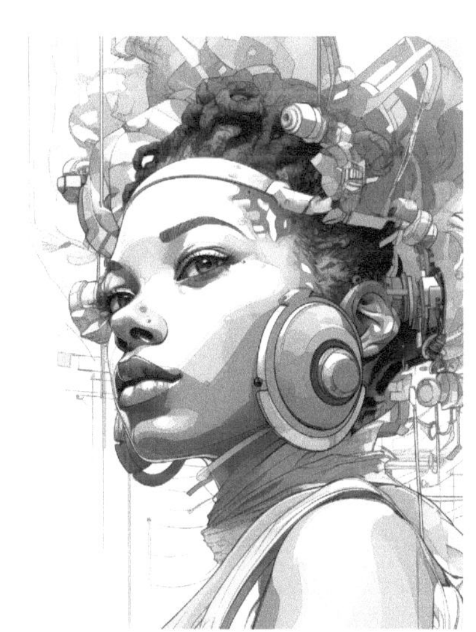
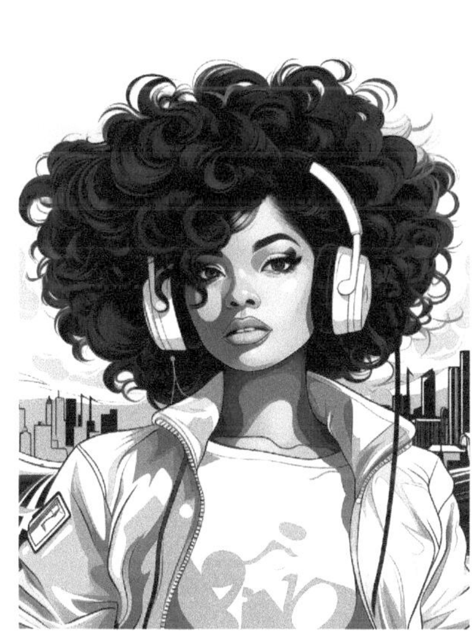
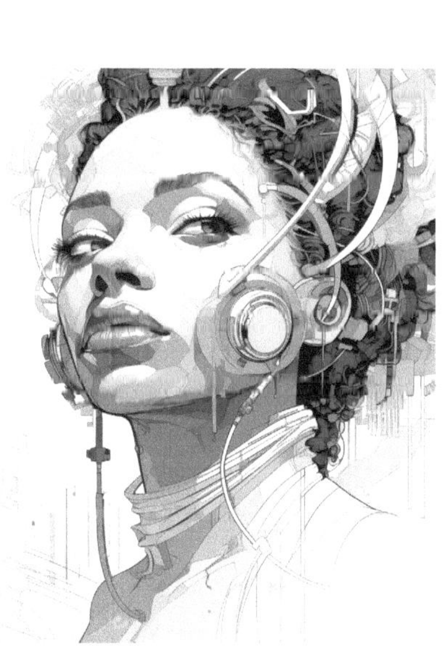

This coloring book is dedicated to the future of Artificial Intelligence. AI has the potential to revolutionize our world and bring about a new era of possibilities. We are only beginning to understand the potential of AI and the possibilities are endless. We hope that this coloring book will inspire the next generation of innovators to explore the possibilities of AI and create a brighter future for us all.

Thank you to all the researchers, scientists, and engineers who have dedicated their lives to advancing the field of AI. Without your hard work and dedication, none of this would be possible.

Finally, we dedicate this coloring book to the future of AI and all the amazing things it will bring.

Sincerely,
The Future of AI Coloring Book Team

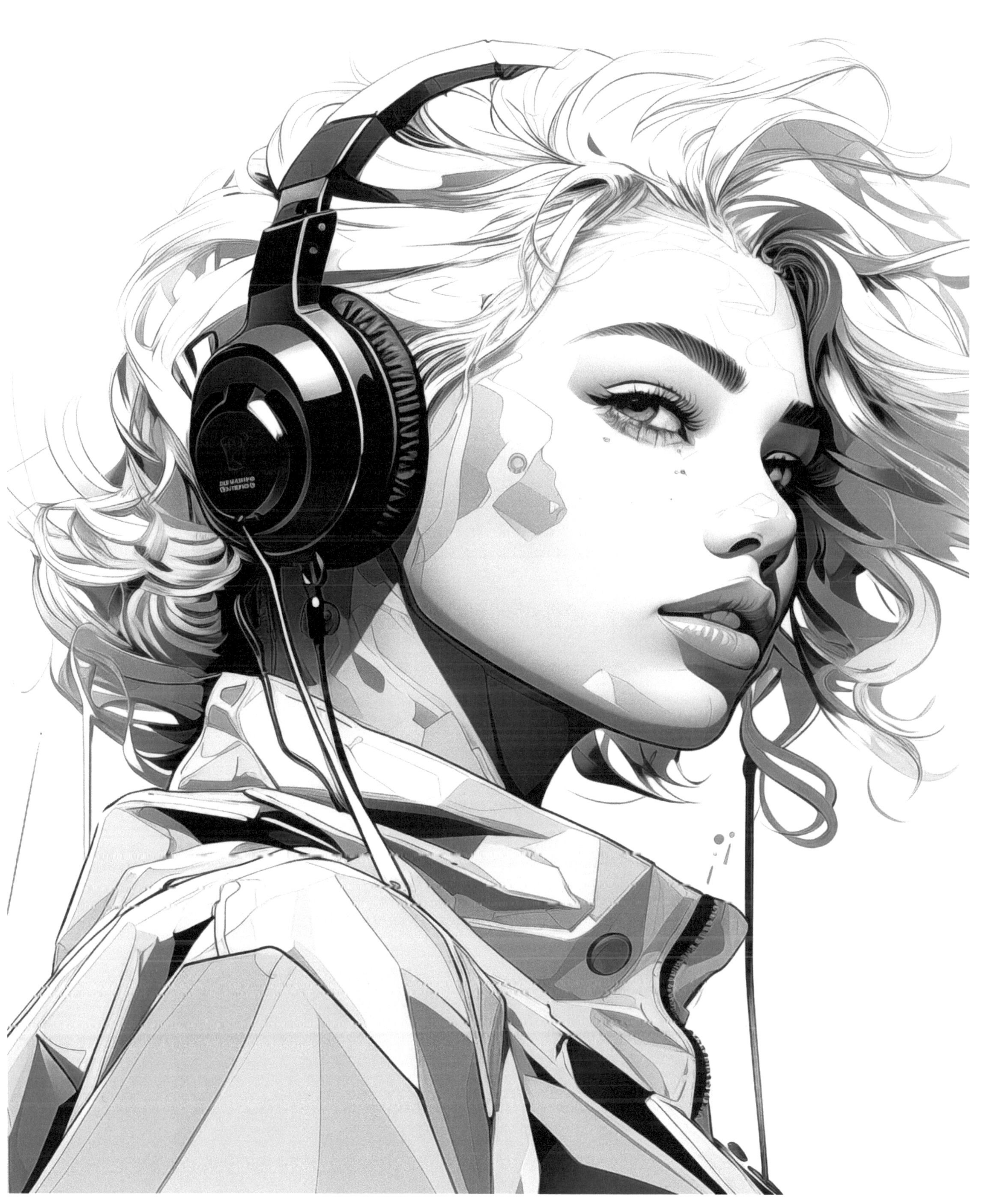

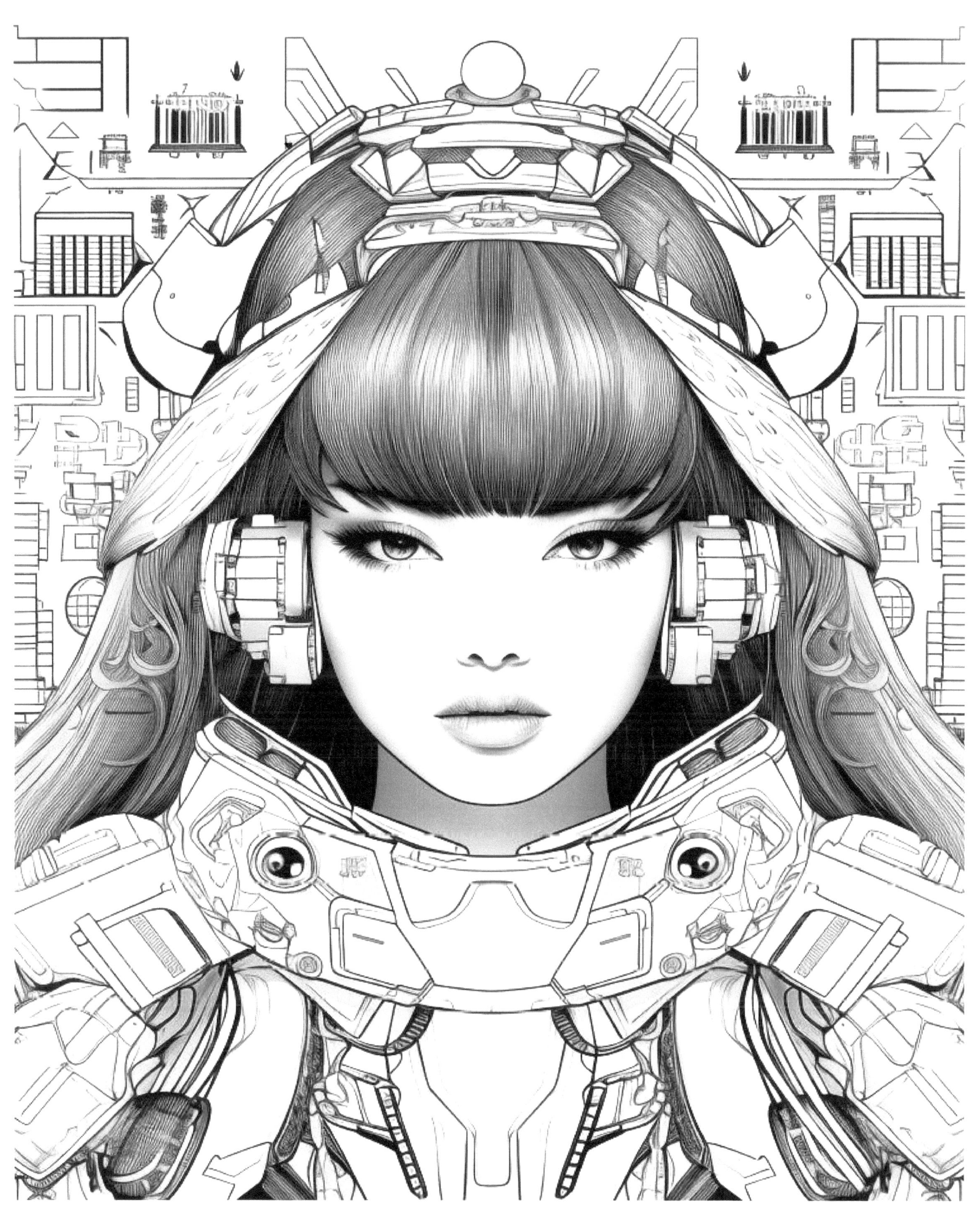

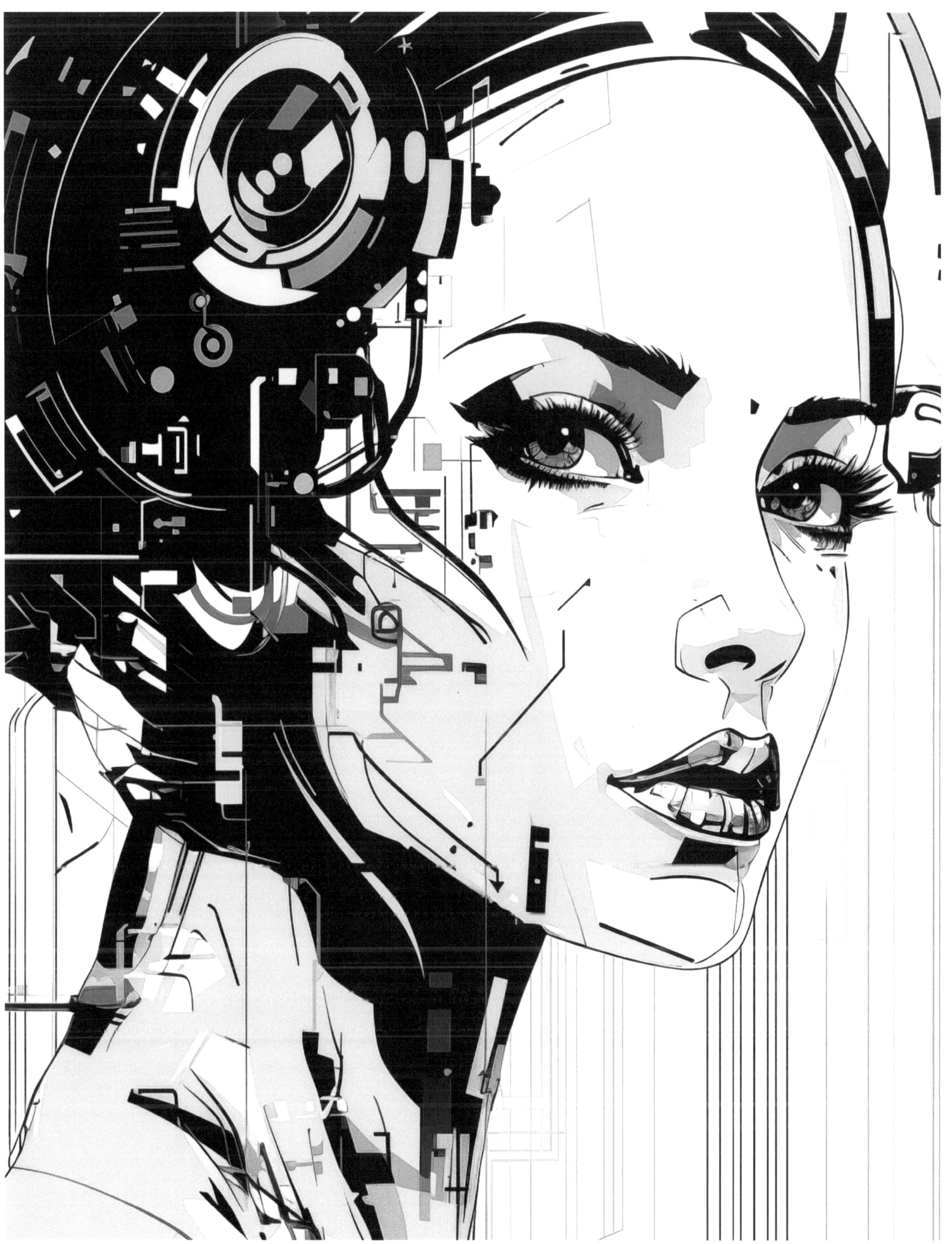

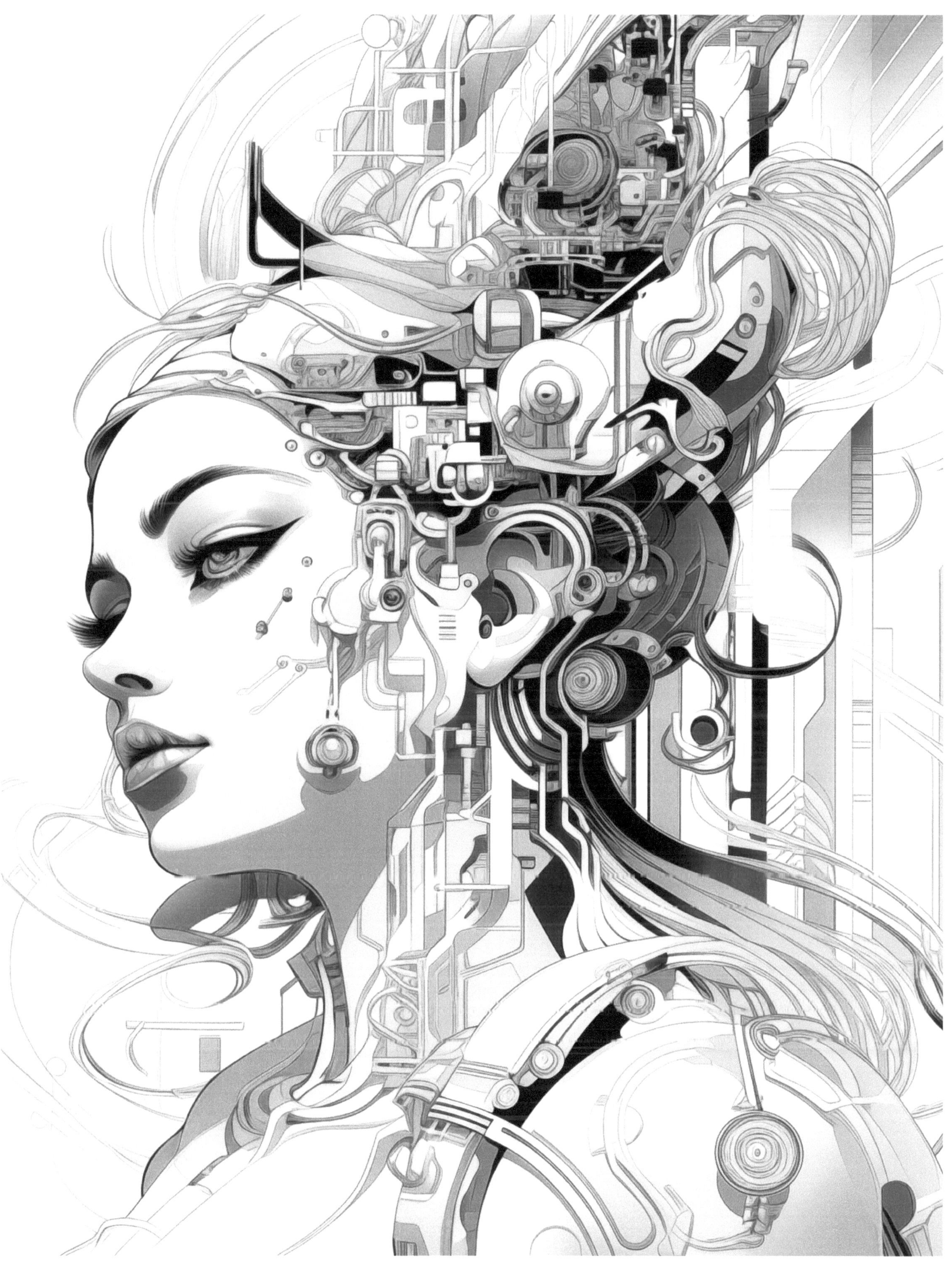

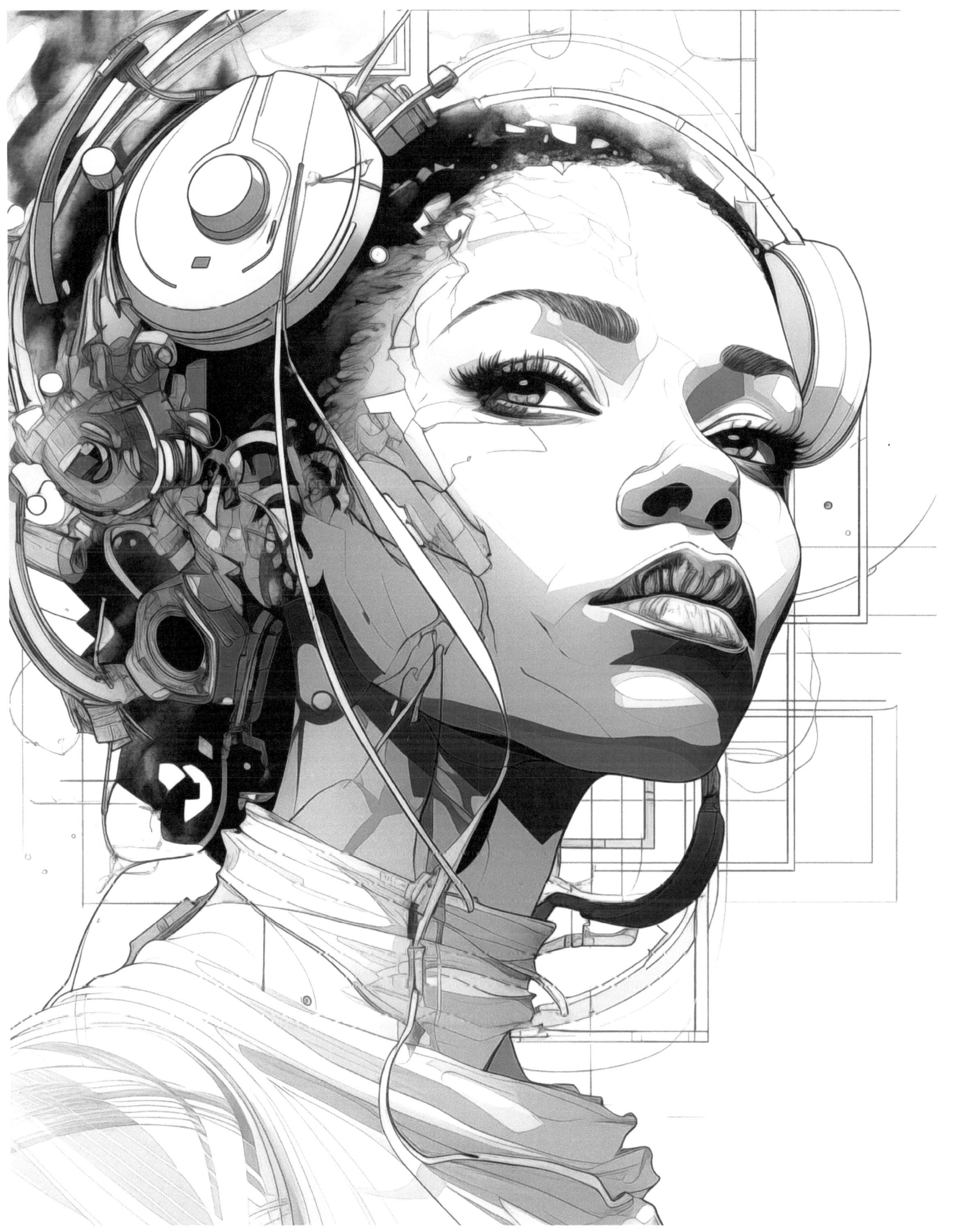

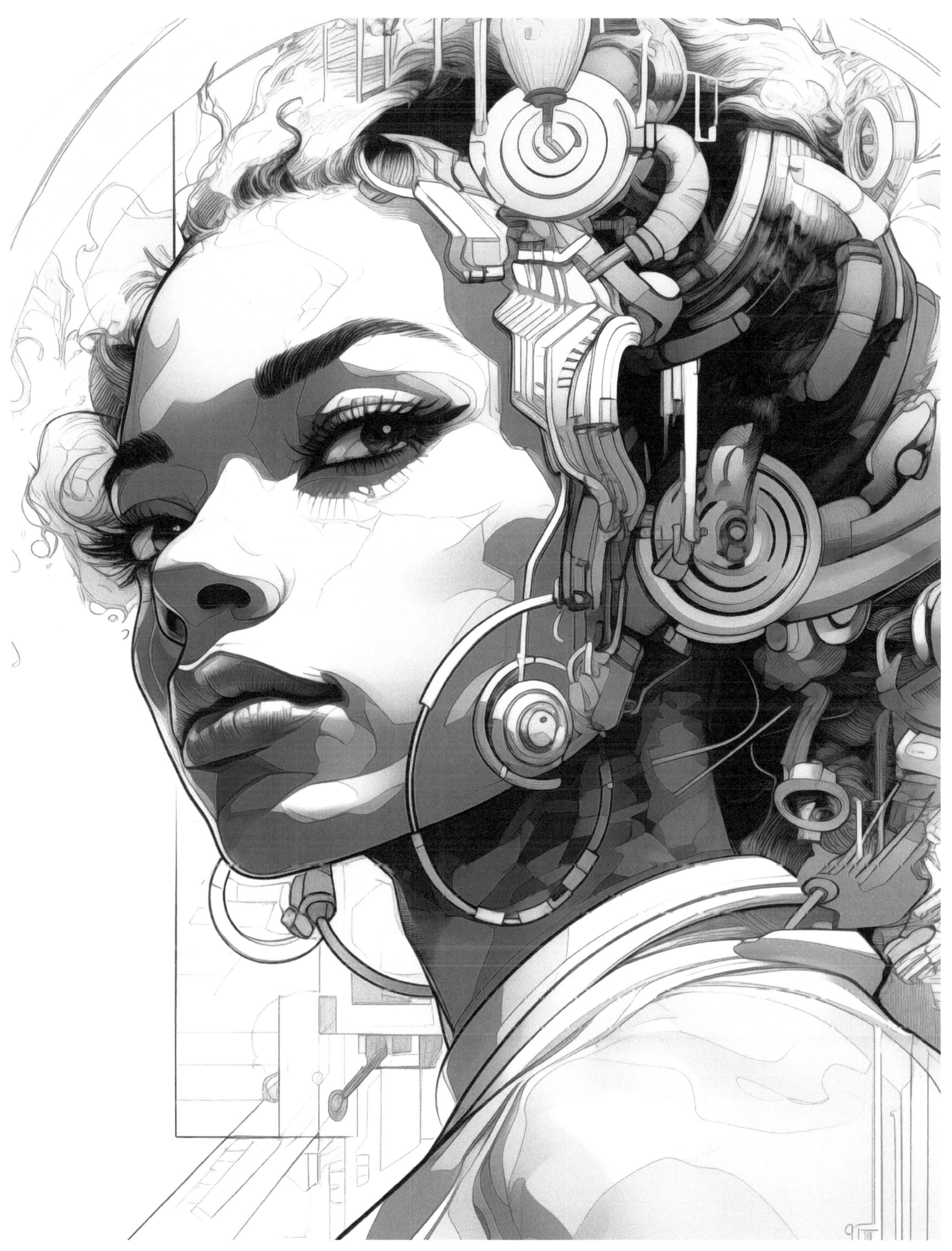

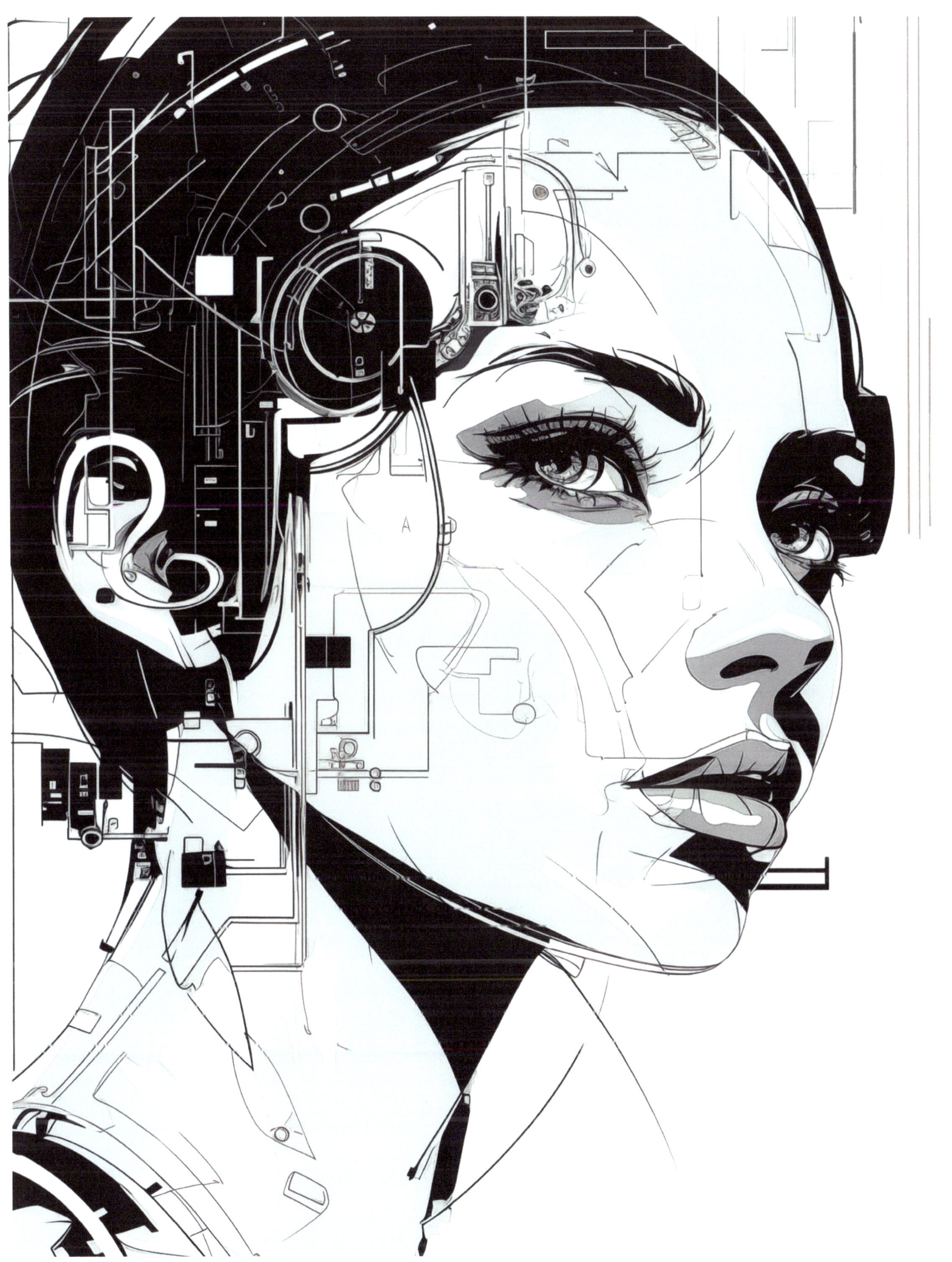

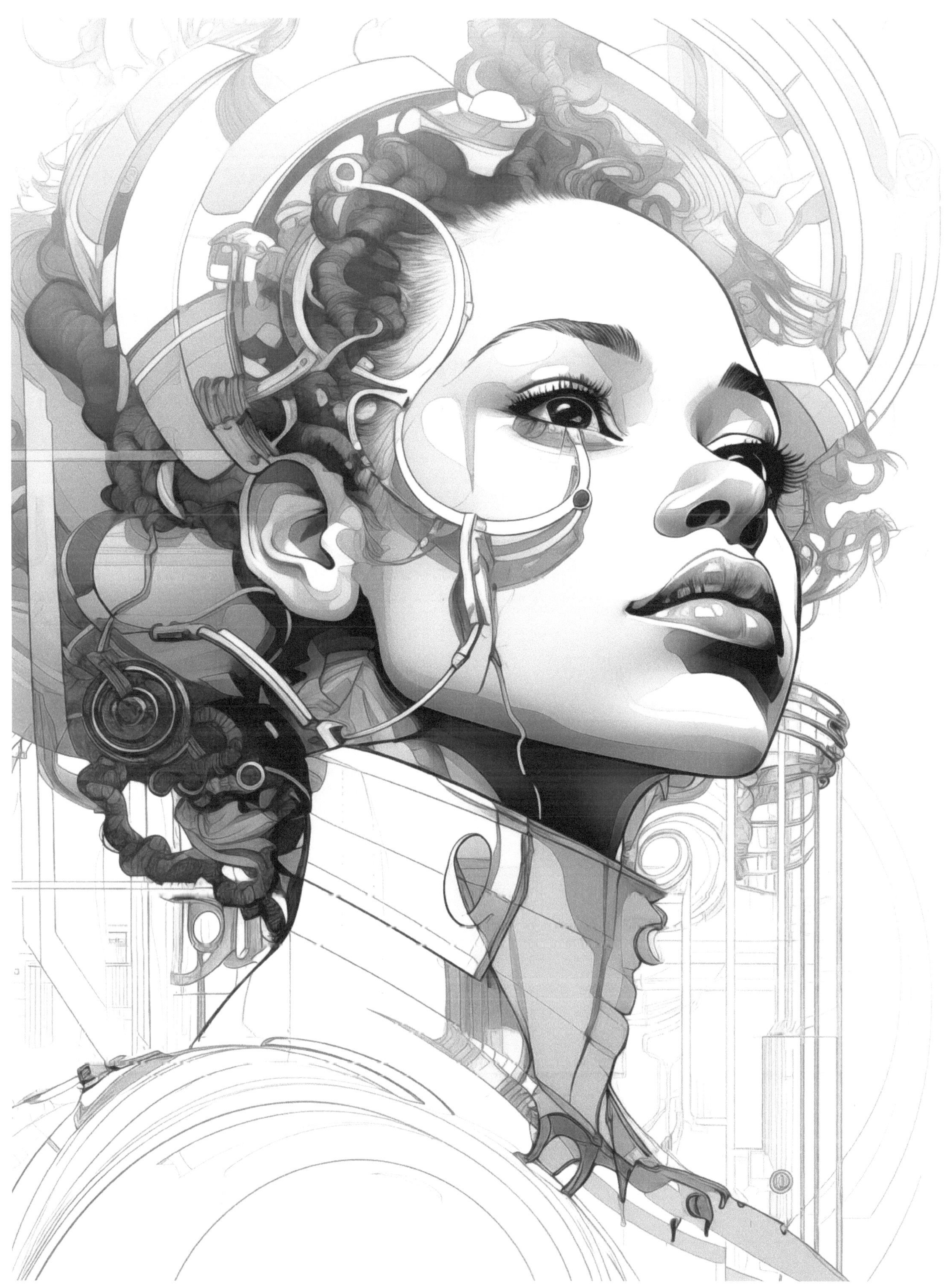

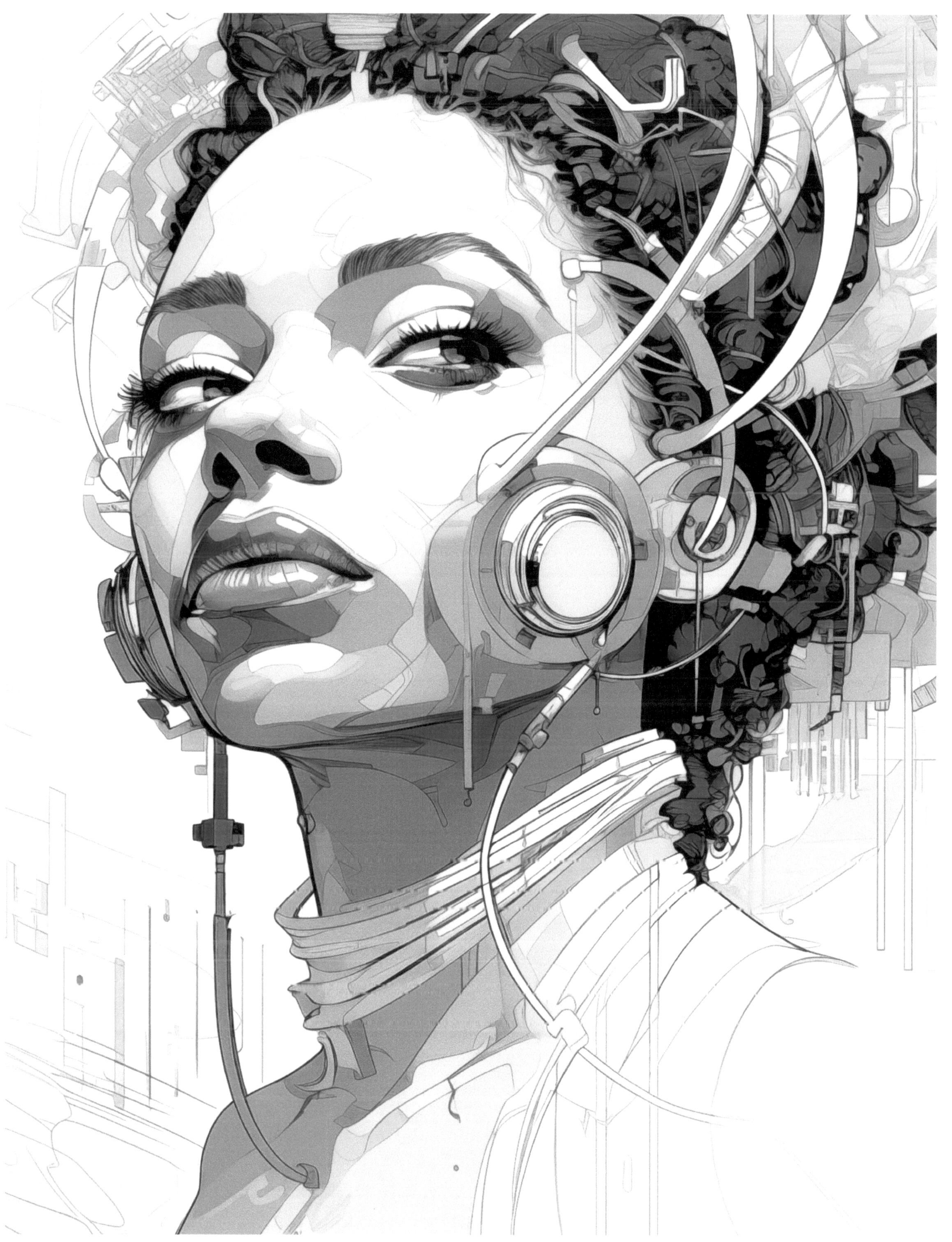

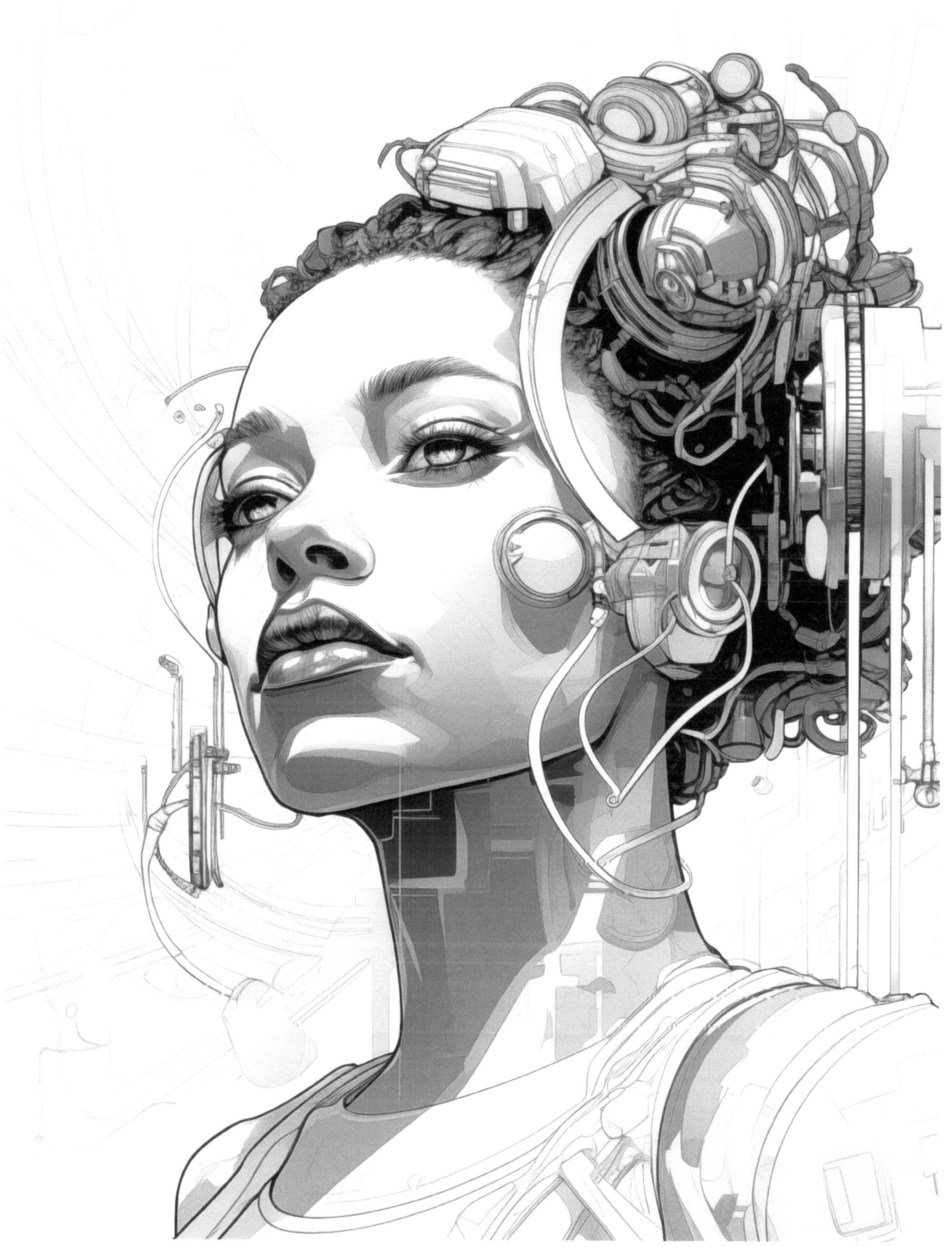

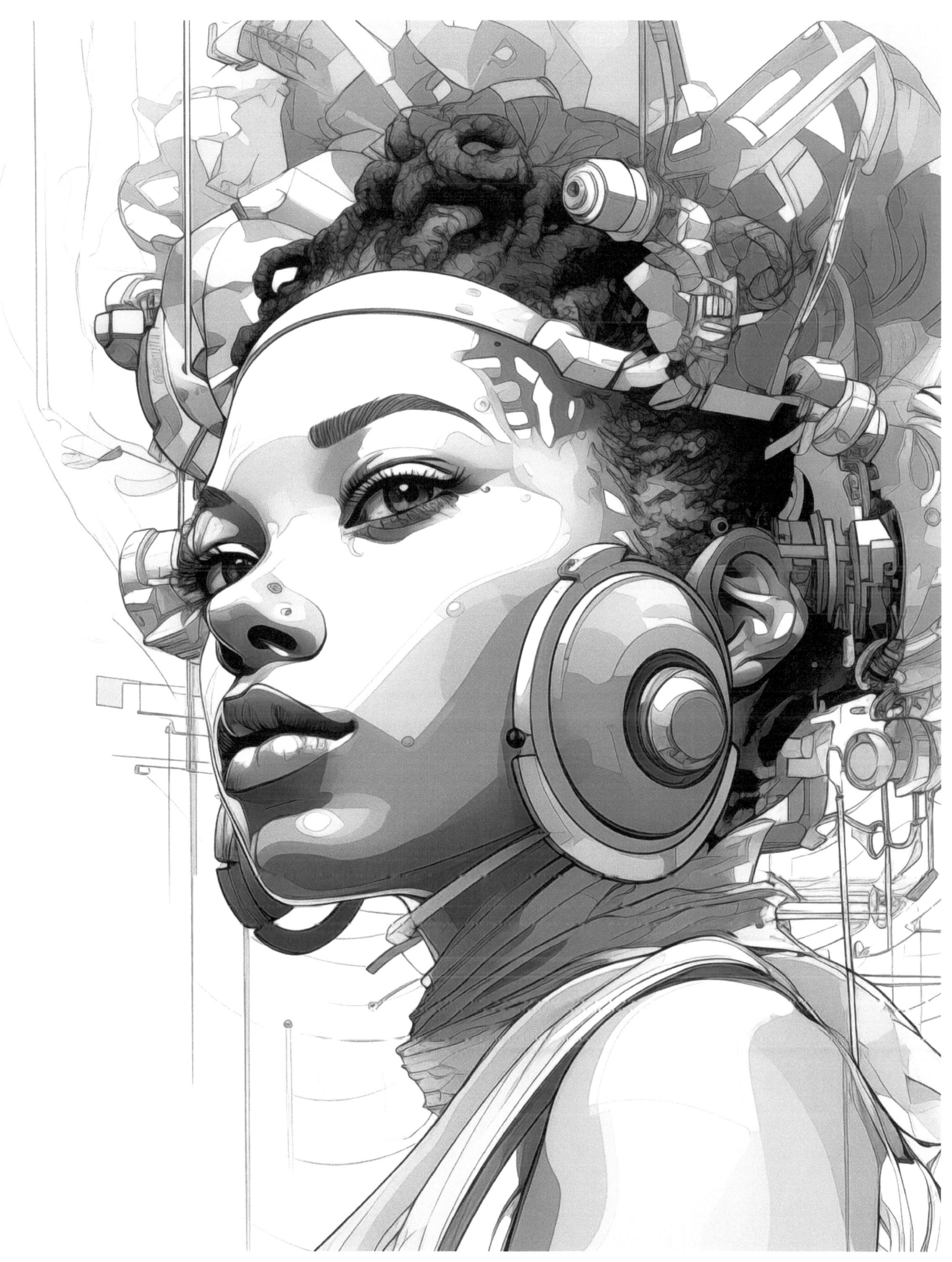

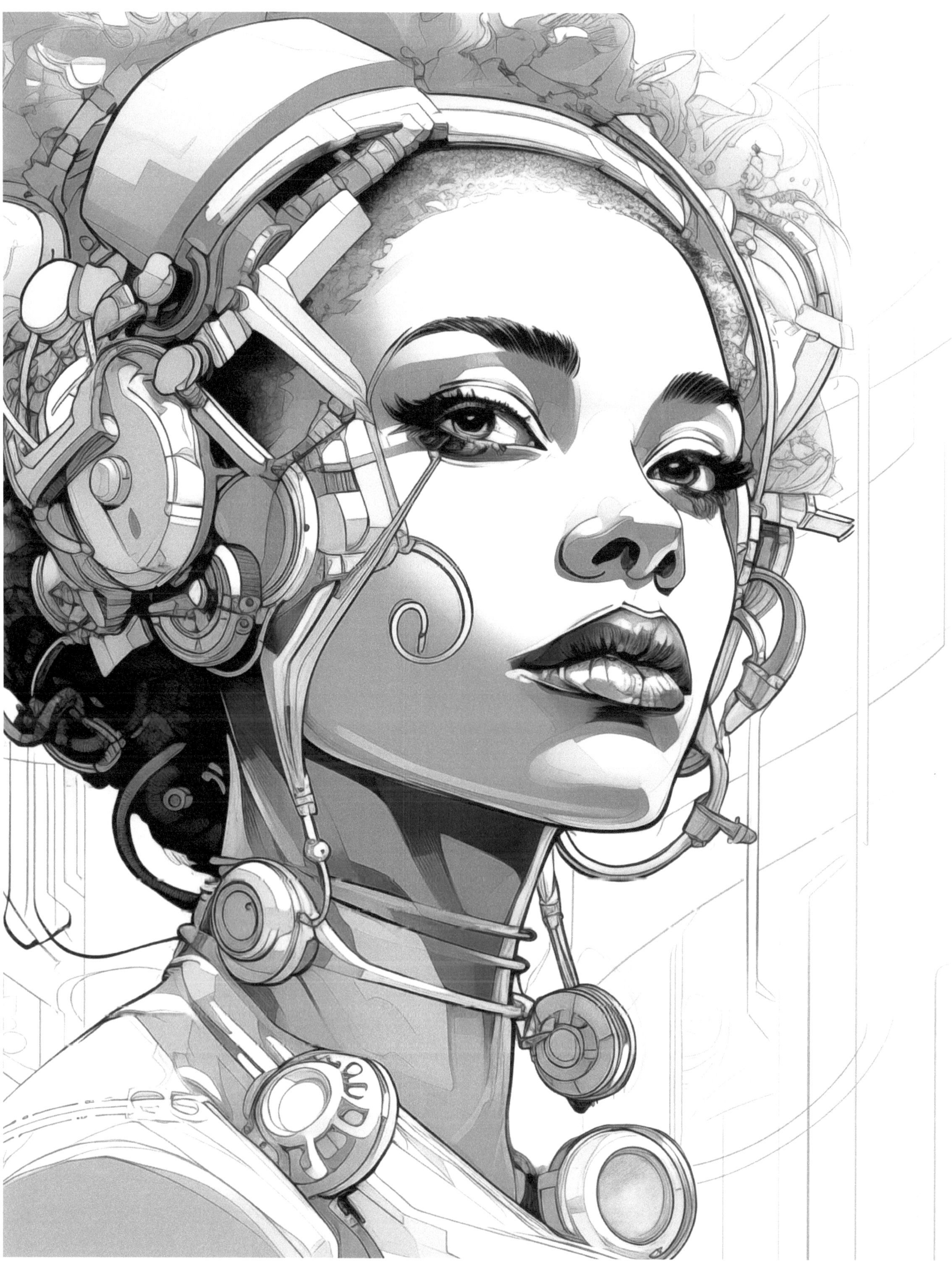

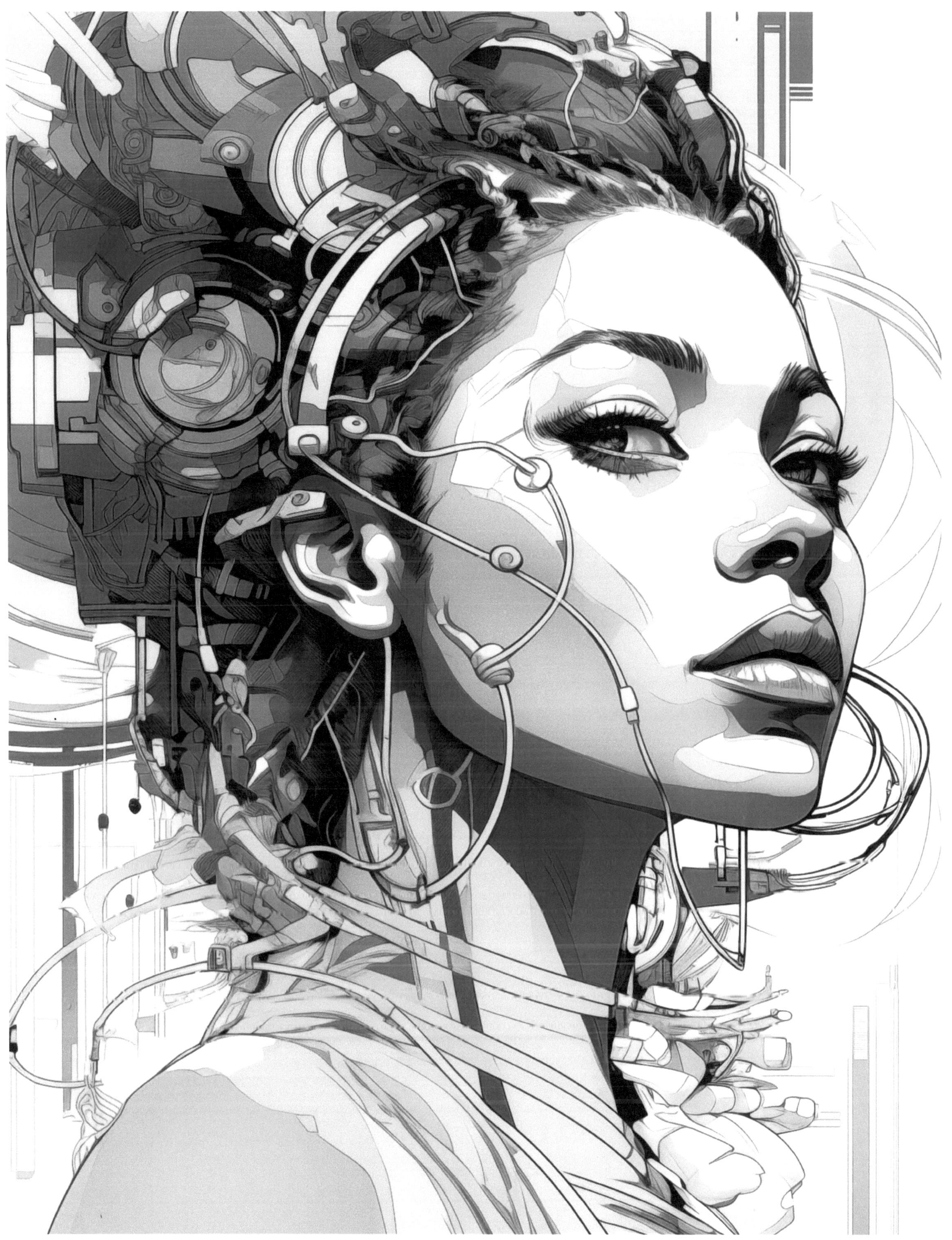

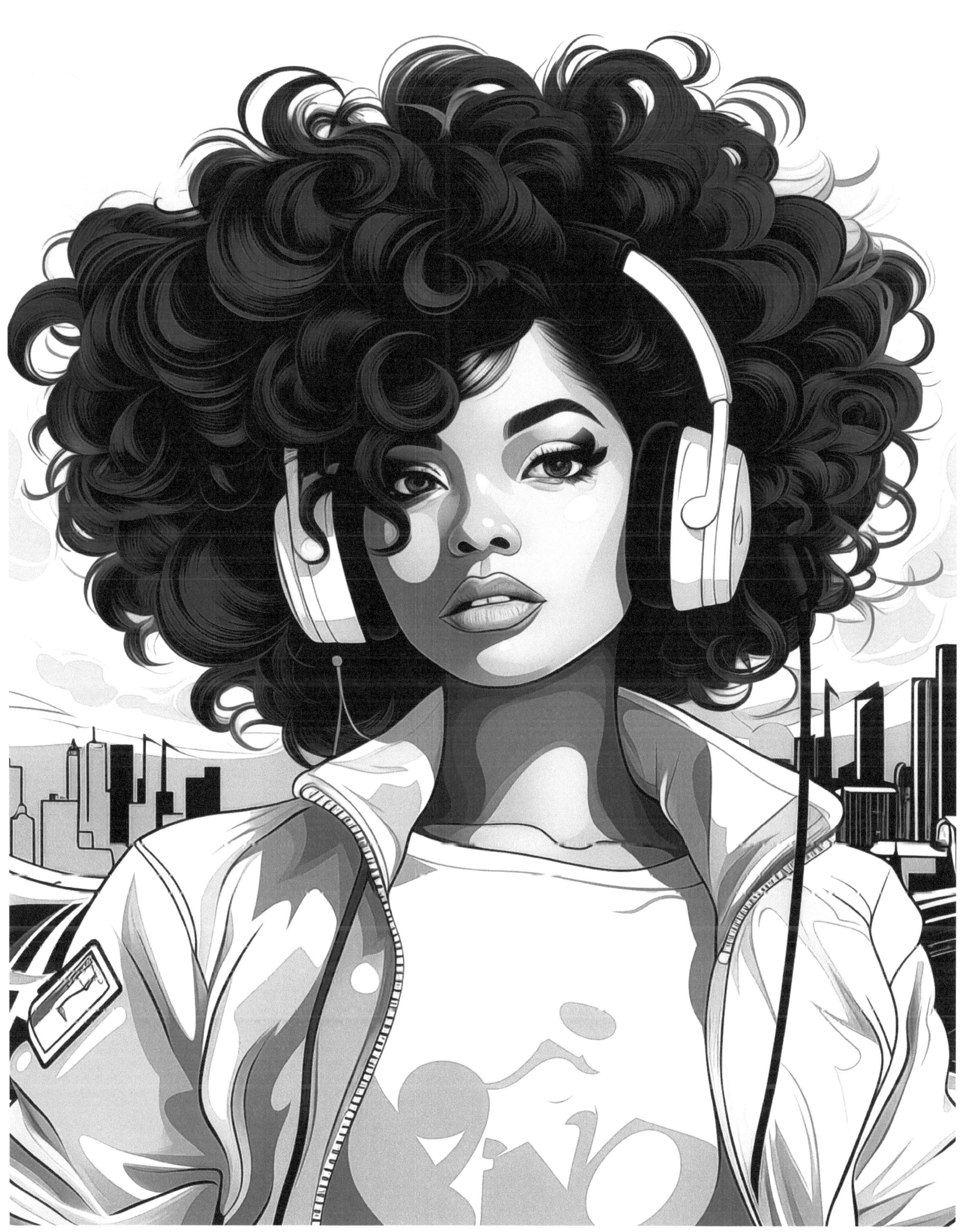

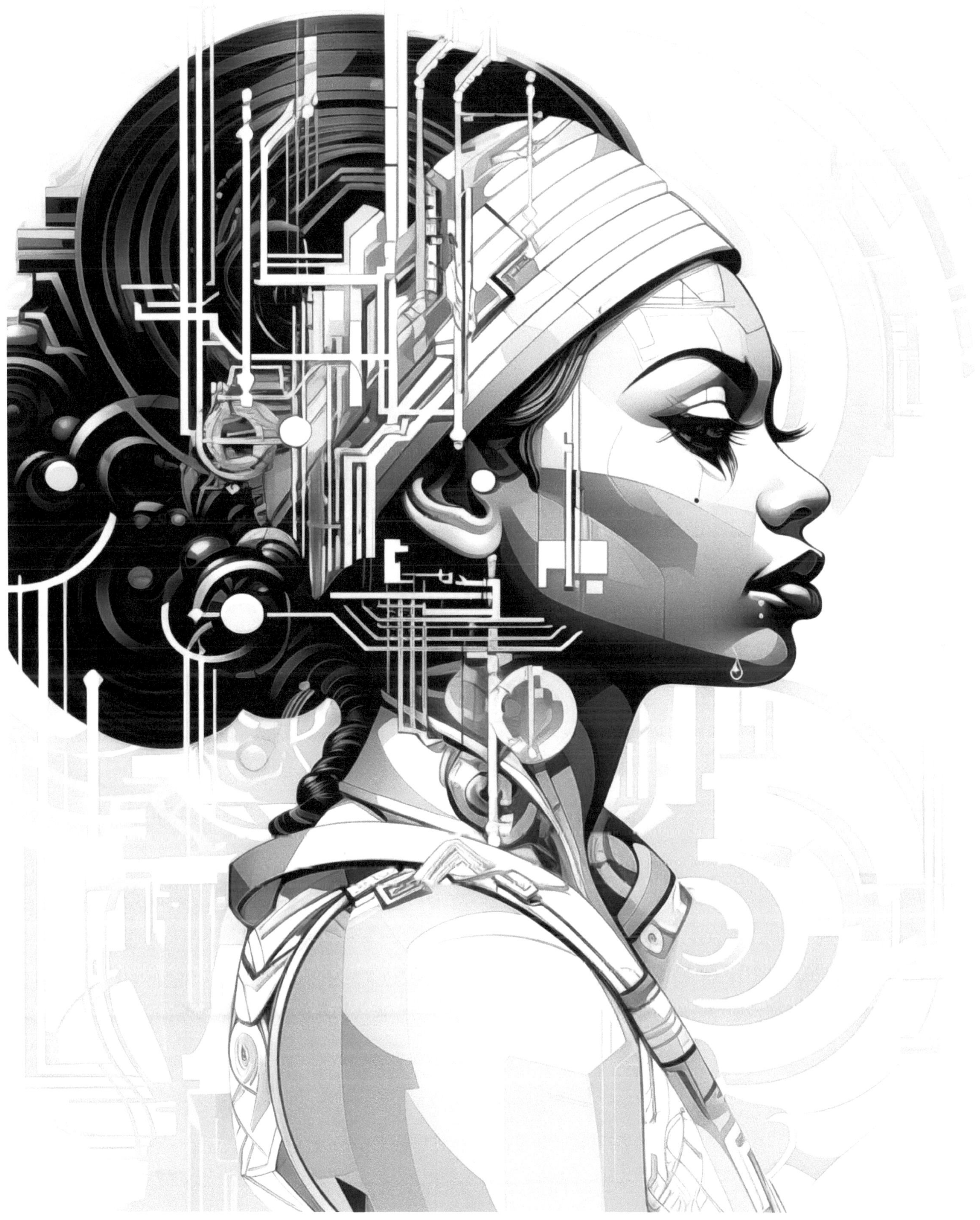

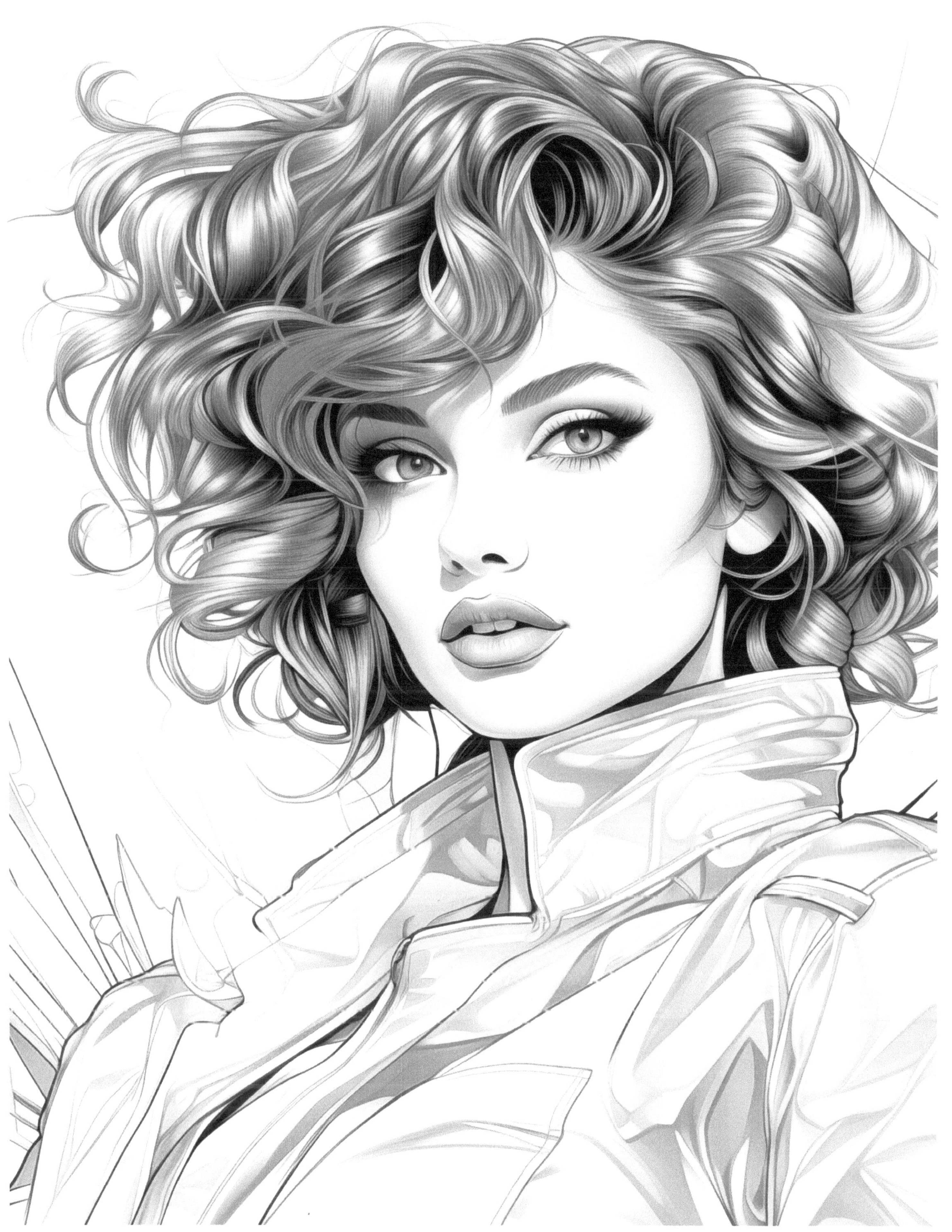

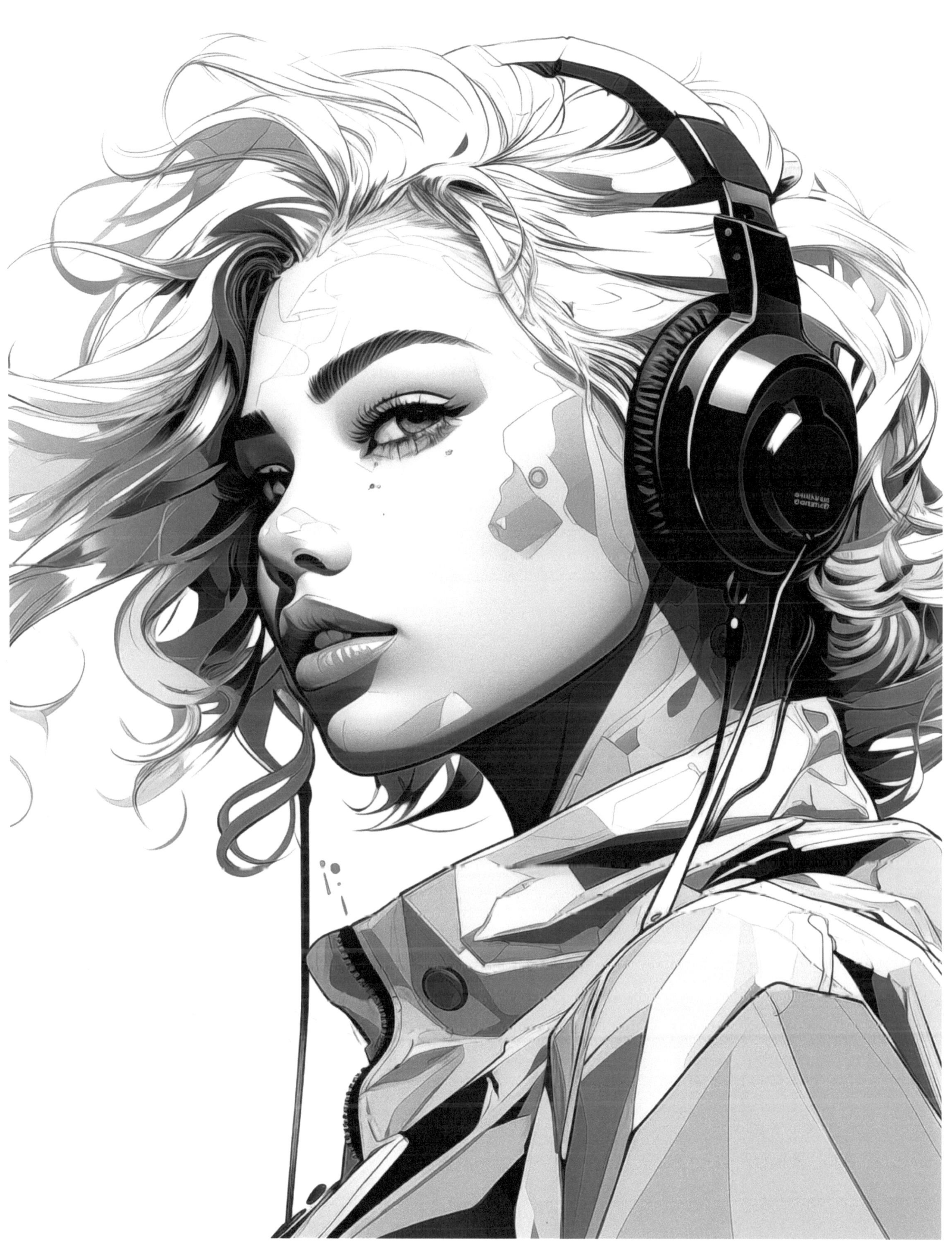

FUTURE

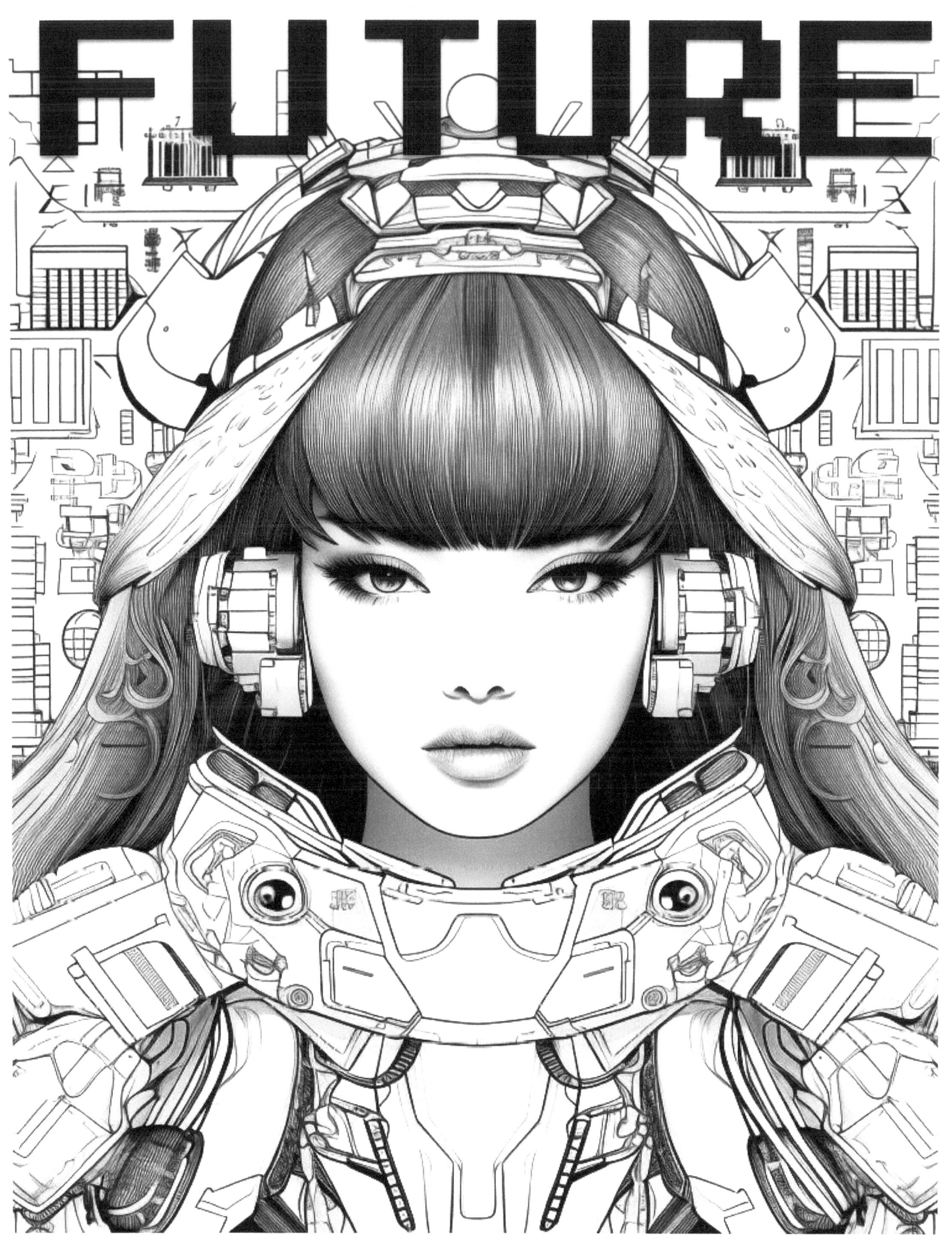